Shropshire
Bath
Oxford
Cambridge
London
Gargoyles and grotesques
The Peak District
Henley on Thames
Guernsey
Jersey
and more

For information on all
our publications see
www.cap-ox.co.uk

CHELTENHAM

A Little Souvenir

CHRIS ANDREWS PUBLICATIONS LTD

CHELTENHAM

The Devil's Chimney and the view from Leckhampton Hill

CHELTENHAM SPA
The most complete Regency town in England.

Cheltenham has been welcoming visitors for nearly three hundred years, ever since the discovery of the first natural spring. The very first Cheltenham Guide of 1781 described a visit to the town as 'a journey of health and pleasure'.

According to legend the first medicinal waters were discovered when pigeons were noticed pecking at salty deposits which had formed around a spring on the present site of Cheltenham Ladies' College. In 1788 King George III came for five weeks to take the water cure; he was followed by many aristocratic and distinguished figures of the period, and Cheltenham's transformation into a fashionable resort began.

Over the following decades the town developed in the architectural style famously popularised by the Prince Regent in Brighton, with sweeping classical terraces and elegant villas set in landscaped estates around broad

6 Cheltenham Town Hall of 1902-3 by local builders Collins and Godfrey

tree-lined walks. It was envisaged by one of its leading developers in 1824 as 'the first English garden city with houses set among formal avenues and gardens', that vision has fortunately been retained: Cheltenham is the most complete Regency town in England - a town specifically designed for leisure and pleasure.

Most of the town centre lies within a conservation area of outstanding national importance; Regency town houses, characterised by the rich patterning of intricate ironwork balconies, surround the leafy

Wishing Fish Clock by Kit Williams in the Regent Arcade   7

Cheltenham Racecourse

10 Pittville lake

Promenade and historic squares. With its colourful, award-winning gardens - survivors from the original Regency pleasure grounds - and impressive range of top quality shops and restaurants, Cheltenham today has a very cosmopolitan ambience which is greatly enhanced by its historic architectural setting.

Cheltenham's heyday as one of England's leading spas lasted from about 1790 to 1840 and it was this period that saw most of the architectural development that survives today. Much of this building was speculative, hence the various 'estates' (the foremost being Pittville, Montpellier and Lansdown) which grew around many of the early spa buildings.

By the mid 19th century Cheltenham was becoming a popular residential town - home to many military families back from service throughout the Empire, the decorative art collections at the Art Gallery & Museum owe much to their generosity. The religious revival of the period also resulted in the building of many neo-Gothic churches and chapels. Their quality reflected not only the wealth of the town but also, in many cases, its connections with those followers of the Arts & Crafts Movement who set up their workshops in the surrounding Cotswold countryside.

12 The Queen's Hotel and Imperial Gardens

Imperial Gardens 13

14 Statue of H M King Edward VII in Montpellier

Montpellier has many unique shops, restaurants and bars   15

16 The buildings on Montpellier Walk are fronted by 'Caryatids' - sculpted figures copied from the Acropolis

18   Floral displays at the top of Montpellier

Shops and St Andrew's Church spire   19

20   The Queen's Hotel overlooking Imperial Gardens

22　Detail of the Ladies' College

Pittville Lake with a temporary exhibit from Sophie Ryder

26   The Promenade

28 Cheltenham's well known Everyman Theatre opened as 'The New Theatre and Opera House' in 1891

Municipal Buildings and floral display on 'The Prom'   29

30 The Wilson, Cheltenham's newly extended Art Gallery & Museum

Edward Wilson was a local man and explorer who accompanied Captain Scott on his expedition to the South Pole

32   Memorabilia in The Wilson includes this haircombe by Fred Partridge from c 1901-6 from the Arts and Crafts Movement collection, and a notable sign

Gustav Holst's Birthplace is also a noted Museum in Cheltenham 33

34　Exterior of the Holst Birthplace Museum

A seasonal attraction, Sandford Lido 35

36   Cheltenham café culture

38   Shopping party or cultural expedition?

Christmas lights and the Promenade 39

Regency architecture in Malvern Road

42 Christ Church, Cheltenham

44 Lansdown Crescent

Lansdown Crescent 45

46   The Chelt in Sandford Park

Gardens off London Road

48   Rooftops in Charlton Kings and the Cotswold escarpment

Tivoli, a compact suburb to the south west of the town   49

50   Cheltenham is increasingly known for its festivals, including music

52   Literature Festival tent

54   Cricket Festival in the grounds of Cheltenham College

Paddy Power
GOLD CUP

1999 THE OUTBACK WAY
2000 LADY CRICKET
2001 SHOOTING LIGHT
2002 CYFOR MALTA
2003 FONDMORT

Cleeve Hill usually overlooks the town from the east

58   Pittville Pump Rooms

Regency ironwork and autumn leaves 59

60   Early spring daffodils enjoy the sun in Montpellier Gardens

Early spring aconites in a domestic garden with snow and sculpture cat   61

62 Cheltenham is surrounded by hills with stunning views

The suburb of Prestbury from Cleeve Hill   63

First published 2007 by Chris Andrews Publications Ltd, revised and updated 2014

15 Curtis Yard North Hinksey Lane Oxford OX2 0LX Telephone: +44(0)1865 723404 **www.cap-ox.com**

Photos: Chris Andrews with additional images from VisitCheltenham/David Sellman, Cheltenham Festival and Angus Palmer
© Chris Andrews Publications Ltd

ISBN 978–1-905385–18-8

Grateful thanks to Angie Rowlands and VisitCheltenham for help, advice and material and to The Wilson Art Gallery &
Museum for permission to include the images on pp 30-33

Front Cover: The Promenade   Title page: Imperial Gardens   Back cover: Pittville Pump Rooms

*This endpaper shows
Cheltenham
The front endpaper
shows the Municipal
Building in
The Promenade*

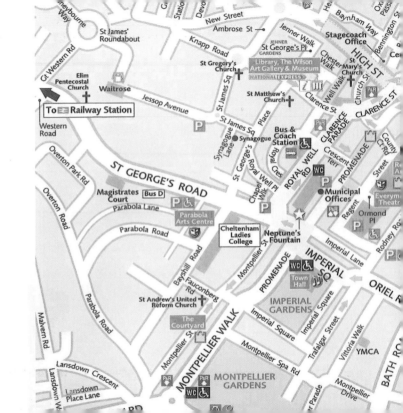